"You've not only given me permission to grieve during this sacred season of letting go, you've given it purpose and filled the void with hope." —*Rebecca H.*

"Thank you for putting into words what my heart has been saying for the past year. I will treasure this book for many years to come." —*Karen S.*

"Beautifully written…hit the nail on the head! A relief to know I'm not alone and not the only crazy mom out there!" —*Debbie S.*

"Laughing…crying...tears running down my face! I've had to face the hard truth that letting go of my eenaged children is not easy. *Release My Grip* meets me in t' s difficult truth and ministers to my mama's heart, remindii me (sometimes in laugh-out-loud ways) that God is walkin̥ right beside me in this crazy time." —*Dawn C.*

"Oh my goodness—it's as though God's hand was in this. I just read this with tears flowing as my daughter is a college sophomore and I am STILL struggling with letting go. Thank you for your words. I feel so blessed to have found this guidance." —*Jean M.*

"Thank you! As a mother of four teens (one in college and one in the midst of the college application process), this was a great reminder that we are not in this journey alone as parents or as students. As our roles shift along the path, God will be with us every step of the way." —*Sue G.*

"This was the most perfect thing I've read as the weeks are coming too fast before my son leaves the nest!" —*Julie O.*

"When my kids left home I was totally unprepared for the 'punch-in-the-gut' feeling of deep loss that I experienced. *Release My Grip* has captured the highs and lows that nobody really talks about when your kids leave home. This should be mandatory reading for dads who have been 'all in' for fatherhood and want some heartfelt wisdom on how to process this enormous change as well as handle this next phase of life as a dad." —*Jon V.*

"Wow, what a blessing to read this. I shed some tears, but I appreciate this glimpse into my future." —*Alan H.*

"I keep forgetting suffering and love go hand and hand, and this helped me make sense of all of the emotions during this season of life. Great reminder of what Christ's love for us looks like." —*Cindy P.*

Kami Gilmour

Release My Grip

*Hope for a Parent's Heart as Kids
Leave the Nest and Learn to Fly*

LIFETREE®
Everyday faith.

Release My Grip: Hope for a Parent's Heart as Kids Leave the Nest and Learn to Fly

Credits

Author: Kami Gilmour

Chief Creative Officer: Joani Schultz

Assistant Editor: Becky Helzer

Designer: Darrin Stoll

Cover Art: Darrin Stoll

Library of Congress Cataloging-in-Publication Data

Names: Gilmour, Kami, 1971- author.
Title: Release my grip : hope for a parent's heart as kids leave the nest and
   learn to fly : /Kami Gilmour.
Description: First American Paperback [edition]. | Loveland, Colorado : Group
   Publishing, Inc., 2017.
Identifiers: LCCN 2016053075 | ISBN 9781470748470 (pbk.)
Subjects: LCSH: Empty nesters--Religious life. | Empty nesters--Family
   relationships. | Adult children--Family relationships.
Classification: LCC BV4529 .G555 2017 | DDC 646.7/8--dc23 LC record available
   at https://lccn.loc.gov/2016053075

ISBN: 978-1-4707-4847-0

10 9 8 7 6 5 4 3 2   25 24 23 22 21 20 19 18 17

Printed in China.

Dedication

To my kids—Faith, Chris, Paige, Nate, and Caleb—
for filling my nest through many seasons
and my heart forever. Fly high!

To my husband, Tim, for keeping me (mostly)
sane through it all. Cheers!

Contents

We tend to get stuck on the "goodbye" part of the story, grieving the image of our kids leaving the nest like it's the final chapter of parenthood. But we forget that our species wasn't born with wings.

Introduction:
A Note From the Author

I first discovered that I was poorly equipped for goodbyes when I was in the third grade and our teacher read our class the book *Charlotte's Web*.

It was such a great story...until the last chapter. My heart jerked up and down the emotional spectrum as Charlotte the spider dies, Wilbur (her BFF pig) faithfully tends to her egg sac, her babies arrive...and then most of the babies end up launching away into the warm spring breeze.

That was the point in the story where I totally lost it. I never even listened to the redemptive conclusion where three babies decide to stay behind; I was too devastated by the horrifying image of five hundred and eleven of Charlotte's babies wafting away and leaving poor Wilbur alone and heartbroken. It was too much grief to bear, and I laid my head down on my desk and sobbed.

Eventually my teacher called the school nurse to escort me out of the classroom because I continued to cry long after story hour was over. I remember the bewildered stares of my classmates as I left the room sniffling and hiccuping uncontrollably, wondering why I was the only one who was so traumatized by the departure of the beloved baby spiders.

More than three decades later, I vividly remembered my *Charlotte's Web* meltdown when I began to feel the pangs of overwhelming grief as my own children prepared to take flight out into the world.

And once again I wondered if I was the only person who experienced such deep heartache with letting go.

I felt alone. And crazy.

After all, it's not like kids growing up and leaving home is a new plot twist to the story of motherhood. I know how the story is supposed to end, and raising capable young adults was always my goal. I had prided myself on my kids' ever-maturing independence, never hovering close enough to be a helicopter parent. I *wanted* them to spread their wings and launch into the world without me.

Or so I thought.

As soon as my daughter, Paige, scheduled her senior pictures the summer before her last year of high school, I began to feel the rumblings of my emotional unraveling.

Where had the time gone?

Wasn't kindergarten just yesterday?

How would I adjust to life without her at home?

I was filled with questions, fears, worries, and wonderings, but I didn't know how to process them. I wished I'd had close friends going through the same thing—or at least been able to find some sort of "postpartum support group" for mothers in transition between these teen and young adult years.

They have those postpartum groups for when we fill our nests; why not when nests empty? Hmmm.

I was terrified something was wrong with me for feeling such deep heartache when I was supposed to be happy.

In the absence of an outlet, I began to journal what was on my heart. And without a person to talk to who I thought would understand, I turned to God.

And something amazing happened.

The pain of this season became holy ground for my own transformational spiritual growth—a catalyst for deepening my relationship with God. *All by default.*

The journaling of my thoughts, fears, and grief became my lamentations—a composition of words from the depth of my soul that I needed to tell God but wasn't yet able to pray.

Writing through my experiences during the season of letting my kids go helped me make sense of things.

It revealed a sacred common thread of truth through each story, and I discovered that a deeper truth seemed to be underlying everything.

I started searching Scripture for more confirmation, and the more I dug in, the clearer God's Word became.

Do not be afraid.

You are not alone.

I am with you.

Trust me, I've got this.

Love never fails.

This is not the end of the story.

These words I heard for myself were the same words I needed to hear on behalf of my children.

Words that promised comfort, hope, peace...and even joy in this season of watching my kids leave the nest and wincing as they learned to fly on their own.

Those words remained the steady rock I could lean on through my kids' senior years, graduations, college drop-offs, and while navigating the ups and downs of their journeys through college.

And as I started to share my stories of learning and letting go on Lifetree's *SoulFeed* blog, I began to hear from thousands of other parents who echoed, *"Me, too."*

As the blog audience grew into millions, I noticed that there are so many other parents who wanted to share their stories of releasing their grip on their growing children as well as reach out and tag friends to give them support on the journey.

To the sweet mom who emailed me the request to "please write a book" along with a picture of a folder containing printouts of blog posts that she'd compiled to help her endure the ride home after college drop-off...*this book is for you.*

And it's for *all* of you who are entering into or already enduring the season of letting go.

The transition our kids make from the teenage years into young adulthood is thrilling and terrifying and often completely perplexing for kids and their parents.

We tend to get stuck on the "goodbye" part of the story, grieving our kids leaving the nest like it's the final chapter of parenthood. But we forget that our species wasn't born with wings. Kids don't exactly launch into the air and fly away forever.

The more accurate picture often looks like this: They sail off on a breeze until they crash into something or the reality of gravity overtakes them, and then they end up on the ground squawking and flopping around awkwardly for a few years until they get their bearings and figure out which direction is up.

Trust me, it usually takes a while. Leaving the nest doesn't happen in a day; it takes place over a season of years. But it's real, it's messy, and it's normal. And if you're struggling (or your kids are struggling) during this time, it doesn't mean you've failed as a parent.

The stories in this book are a collection of "aha" moments I journaled while standing knee-deep in the season of releasing my grip as my daughter left the nest followed by my son a few years later.

I hope the experiences I'm sharing with you offer encouragement, hope, and the wisdom learned in hindsight. (And if you're feeling like an imperfect mother, at least you'll realize you've got company!)

Following many chapters, you'll also find a devotional section with relevant Scripture passages and reflection questions along with journaling space. They're there so you can process and record your own experiences on your journey and draw closer to God with renewed strength.

And I hope you'll hang on to this book to reflect on what you've written after you've walked the path awhile...it might become a treasured keepsake to remind you how God showed up in this season of life.

It turns out we *can* get through this.

We're not crazy, and we're certainly not alone. We're all in this together.

But just in case you're not convinced, feel free to take the quiz "18 Signs Your Kid Is Graduating and Leaving the Nest and You're Totally Losing It" in the next section to confirm that you are part of this tribe of parents who are on the same path.

Quiz:

18 Signs Your Kid Is Graduating and Leaving the Nest and You're Totally Losing It

If you're like me, you never paid much attention to senior year hoopla until you realized that *this* is the year that will adorn your child's tassel charm on their high school graduation cap.

Now that you've accepted the reality, you're probably wandering around in a complex emotional state that ranges from pride to panic. And all the while you're utterly perplexed by how fast the time has gone by.

Hang in there—you're not alone, and you're not crazy.

But in case you're not convinced, here's a checklist of 18 common traits that mark every parent's journey through the temporary insanity during this season of life from senior year to college drop-off.

❑ 1. You've turned into mom-parazzi—obsessed with taking photos and videos of your child throughout senior year because you're haunted by the fact that you haven't actually completed a photo album since their first year of life.

❑ 2. You suddenly feel guilty for EVER missing one of their sporting events and have vowed to attend EVERY SINGLE game this spring—even the "away" games. (Even the very far away games.)

❑ 3. You contemplate setting things on fire while trying to navigate the online FAFSA process (a.k.a. the eighth circle of hell).

❑ 4. You're fanatically savoring their "lasts"—their last Easter at home, last prom, last practice, last game, last band concert, and their last awards banquet.

❑ 5. There's a box of graduation announcements sitting on the dining room table, but You. Can't. Even. Go. There.

❑ 6. You've become that person who wistfully advises parents of young children to enjoy every moment because it goes by so very, very fast.

❑ 7. You stare at the atrocity of their bedroom, deeply concerned for their lack of laundry competence but secretly thrilled that they'll soon have to face this challenge on their own.

❑ 8. You start panicking and make a list of essential life skills you still need to teach them.

❑ 9. You torment yourself by starting a mental countdown of the weeks and days until they leave as if it's an execution date or something equally grim.

❑ 10. You get super-clingy and follow your kid around the house, asking to hang out every waking moment of the day.

❑ 11. You find yourself lurking in a dark corner of their bedroom, watching them sleep.

❑ 12. You take some stealth measurements of their bedroom and wonder how long you need to wait after they leave before it's OK to turn it into a home gym.

❑ 13. You find that random things make you burst into tears: childhood photos, a stack of empty boxes and packing tape outside their room, their dirty cereal bowl left on the counter…the first glance at their tuition bill.

❑ 14. You stalk your kid's future college roommate on social media, trying to determine if there's any possibility this space-sharing stranger could be a sex-crazed, shoplifting, nocturnal, meth-cooking psychopath with poor hygiene or bad study habits.

❑ 15. Your nesting instinct goes into overdrive, and you realize you've spent more on dorm room essentials than on an entire semester of college room and board.

❑ 16. You appear somewhat unstable while emphatically trying to convince your eye-rolling college student that they will certainly need such dorm essentials as a day planner, umbrella, rain boots, sewing kit, and that armchair-backrest pillow thingy that's existed for three decades.

❑ 17. You go through an entire box of tissues one night while looking through decades of old photos—including ones from your own college days—and wonder how all of these glorious years went by so fast and how you could possibly be this old.

❑ 18. You suddenly realize the age you somehow thought you still were is the age your kid has now become.

If you checked four or more of the signs from the list, welcome to the club. You're finally beginning to embrace the journey of truly letting them go.

And though it may feel as if sending your young adult off to college or out into the world is the final curtain call of parenthood, I promise you that it's not.

This time is not just about a season that's ending; it's about a new season that's just beginning.

For them, and for you as well.

Just keep reminding yourself that, for everyone, the best is yet to come.

Part 1:
Leaving the Nest

"Like an eagle that stirs up its nest, that flutters over its young, spreading out its wings, catching them, bearing them on its pinions" Deuteronomy 32:11. (ESV)

Lord, please **give me the strength** to celebrate this milestone without ugly crying during graduation. I'd prefer not to show up in family photos of this special day with a streaky/red/puffy/post-meltdown face.

Chapter 1

Give Me the Strength:
A Parent's Prayer
at Graduation

Spring 2016

Lord, have mercy.

There's a cap and gown hanging in my son's room, and it's taking my breath away.

He's graduating soon, and I can't believe how fast the time has gone. Did you maybe spin the earth a little faster on its axis for the past several years?

He's ready…but I'm not sure if I am.

Because since the day he was born and wrapped his tiny fingers around mine, my heart has been living outside of my body. At that moment I understood the concept of unconditional love—including your love.

Thank you for making me his mom…and trusting my hands to care for this little human's life when I had no clue what I was doing.

This parenting journey has been the hardest, funniest, stinkiest, most terrifying, inspiring, holy mess…and there are a lot of parts I messed up that I wish I could do over.

Please forgive me for the times I was exhausted and bitter and wanted to give up. Forgive me for yelling a lot. Forgive me for not paying attention. Forgive me for forgetting things. Forgive me for dropping off my 6-year-old son and leaving him unsupervised for three hours at the sketchy roller rink because I had the date wrong for his friend's birthday party. Forgive me for all of the mistakes I made as his mom.

And please help him forget this stuff—or at least help him forgive me if my failures screwed him up. Hopefully you can turn the consequences into something positive—like the development of grit and resilience.

Thank you for the sweet moments, too—there were so many of those. The baby snuggles, the funny toddler sayings, the little boy hugs, the sloppy Mother's Day craft gifts and Popsicle-stick Christmas ornaments that I can't ever throw away, the hoopla of snow days, the sight of 10 pairs of sneakers in the doorway and the house packed with friends, the camaraderie of other parents on the sidelines of at least a thousand soccer and baseball games, the family road trips, the conversations around the dinner table, and sitting on his bed whenever I still remember to tuck him in at night…this is what I'll miss.

But most of all, I'm going to miss him in the ordinariness of the everyday. Because being by his side and watching him grow up for the past 18 years— on the good days and the bad—has been the greatest joy and privilege of my life.

Oh Lord, release my grip and give me the courage to let him go. (You're gonna have to pry my fingers back a little.)

Remind me that he is yours…that he's always been yours.

Remind me that you'll be with him, especially when he feels alone.

Remind me that your love for him is even bigger than mine.

Remind me that I've done my best to raise a young man who follows you.

Remind me that letting him go is a much better alternative to letting him live in my basement forever.

And while you're at it, please remind him of all of the above, too.

Lastly, Lord, please give me the strength to celebrate this milestone without ugly crying during graduation. I'd prefer not to show up in family photos of this special day with a streaky/red/puffy/post-meltdown face.

Because I want him to know that I'm more proud than sad. I want him to know that I'm more excited about what's next than afraid. I want him to know that I believe in him.

And I want him to know that I believe in you.

Lord, in your mercy, hear my prayer.

P.S. Please keep the rain away during our graduation open house celebration, because I forgot to rent a tent and 150+ people are just not going to fit inside our home.

Digging Deeper—Devotions and Journaling

Find a quiet place where you can relax and listen to what Jesus has to say to you.

If you're experiencing the emotions of graduation season, what words do you have for God? Journal your own prayer here.

_____

_____

_____

_____

_____

_____

_____

_____

_____

_____

_____

_____

_____

_____

_____

_____

_____

_____

_____

_____

_____

I've realized the secret to surviving my kids **leaving the nest** is to be fully present to support them and look forward to the future through the lens of their life, not backward through the lens of my life.

Chapter 2

For Everything
There Is a Season

"...and a time to every purpose under heaven."

Spring 2013 and Spring 2016

When my daughter, Paige, entered her senior year of high school, I was a complete train wreck.

Seriously: I. Was. Not. OK.

I couldn't fathom how the years had slipped away so quickly and we were already approaching this huge milestone.

I desperately wanted time to slow down to delay the inevitable "last-time moments."

I wandered through her entire senior year with tear-fogged eyes, paralyzed by grief at the thought of letting her go. I even quit my job so I could try to make up for all of the moments I'd missed.

Nostalgia was my nemesis, and I was tormented by my constant reflection of the past.

Memories of my daughter growing up repeated in my head like clips from a sappy movie, culminating in visions of the farewell scene as we dropped her off at college. *Would we be in her dorm room? Would we be driving away watching her in the rearview mirror as she waved from the residence hall steps? Would she cry? Would her dad cry? Would I even be able to breathe?*

So I cried through Paige's entire senior year. And then I ugly cried through graduation, during her college orientation that summer, in the checkout line at Target when we bought things for her dorm, and as we packed up her boxes and loaded the car.

And when the moment I'd been dreading finally arrived, I ugly cried so hard as I hugged her one last time in the parking lot of her quad and said goodbye.

Of course I also cried the whole way home…and every time I walked by her empty bedroom for a few weeks after she'd left.

But gradually the crying ceased.

That day of letting go had come and gone, and I had survived.

But more importantly, my daughter had survived leaving home, and she was thriving in college. She loved her new friends, her classes, the campus life, and the freedom of this new season.

Fast forward several years to now—she's a junior in college and studying abroad next semester, and soon her brother will be graduating from high school and heading off to college in the fall.

And here's the shocker: I'm not having a full-blown nuclear meltdown this time. (At least not yet.)

I've realized the secret to surviving my kids leaving the nest is to be fully present to support them and look forward to the future through the lens of their life, not backward through the lens of my life.

I'd been so preoccupied by the suffocating vice grip of mama-mourning what I was "losing" that I hadn't paid much attention to how exciting this new phase of life was going to be for her.

Truth? This season is about them—not about me. (OK, everything with my kids is still a little bit about me, but it's not *my* spotlight.)

Watching my daughter grow into the amazing young woman she's becoming during college has been a true joy. She's had ups and downs during these years, but it's been evident how her independence has helped her grow into her true self.

Remembering this helps me come back to what is real and what is now—and find relief in being present in this sweet season of her young adult life as I put my trust in God's plans for her future.

I'm not beating myself up for feeling the pains of letting go—because they are real and it is hard to embrace this transition. I will never make it through these times without some breakdowns. But I don't want my tears to overshadow milestones that deserve to be celebrated with joy and pride.

And now it's my son's turn.

As Nate's high school graduation and college departure looms ahead on the calendar, I refuse to torment myself with visions of our last goodbye when we drop him off at his dorm.

And I refuse to twist the memories of his chubby toddler hands cupping my face as he professed his love for me "to the moon and back" into a motherhood meltdown where I am stuck in grief, longing for days gone by.

I love him, I believe in him, and I'm excited for him—so this time around I'll focus my heart on savoring the details of those last few months with him as well as visions of him thriving in college and growing into a wonderful adult I can't wait to get to know better.

As Nate leaves the nest, letting go of him will be tough. But he'll be back. And then he'll leave again. And again. This season of young adulthood will adopt a new normal with the rhythm of coming and going.

What I know for sure as a veteran mother of a graduating kid is this simple truth: *The finish line is just a myth.*

Parenthood is a lifelong journey—and it's also a lifelong (often painful) practice of letting one season go as a new season begins.

It begins postpartum and doesn't end on our kid's 18th birthday...or their high school graduation...or when they leave for college...or when they graduate from college...or when they get married...or even when they become parents themselves.

Parenthood will never be over, and God will never be done with them.

It'll just be a different season.

And I want to be present for it.

Digging Deeper—Devotions and Journaling

Find a quiet place where you can relax and listen to what Jesus has to say to you about clinging to the past as a new season begins for your child.

As you look back on your past, read and reflect on the following Bible verses:

> "But forget all that—it is nothing compared to what I am going to do. For I am about to do something new. See, I have already begun! Do you not see it? I will make a pathway through the wilderness. I will create rivers in the dry wasteland" Isaiah 43:18-19. (NLT)

> "Don't long for 'the good old days.' This is not wise" Ecclesiastes 7:10. (NLT)

Ask Jesus the following question (even if you think you know the answer), and journal his response to you: *What moments from my past are stealing the peace of my present?*

As you consider your future, read and reflect on the following verses from the Bible:

> *"How do you know what your life will be like tomorrow? Your life is like the morning fog—it's here a little while, then it's gone" James 4:14. (NLT)*

> *" 'For I know the plans I have for you,' declares the Lord, 'plans to prosper you and not to harm you, plans to give you hope and a future' " Jeremiah 29:11. (NIV)*

Create two lists, one for "Fears" and the other for "Hopes."

Journal everything that comes to mind as you consider these two questions:

- *What are your fears about the future—for yourself, and for your family?*

_____

_____

_____

_____

_____

_____

_____

_____

_____

_____

- *What are your hopes and dreams about the future—for yourself, and for your family?*

As you consider your present—this time of letting go—read and reflect on the following passage from the Bible:

"There is a time for everything, and a season for every activity under the heavens:

a time to be born and a time to die,
a time to plant and a time to uproot,
a time to kill and a time to heal,
a time to tear down and a time to build,
a time to weep and a time to laugh,
a time to mourn and a time to dance,

a time to scatter stones and a time to gather them,
a time to embrace and a time to refrain from embracing,
a time to search and a time to give up,
a time to keep and a time to throw away,

a time to tear and a time to mend,
a time to be silent and a time to speak,
a time to love and a time to hate,
a time for war and a time for peace"
Ecclesiastes 3:1-8. (NIV)

Ask Jesus the following question (even if you think you know the answer), and journal what he reveals: **Who or what needs my attention in this present season of life?**

Up for a Challenge?

Look over what you've written about your past...future...and present. Spend time in prayer asking Jesus to reveal his perfect peace in your present situation as you surrender your burdens from the past and trust him with your fears about the future.

Release my grip

when I hug him one last
time and I don't want
to let go, and remind
me I've raised a young
man who's ready to
spread his wings.

Chapter 3

Release My Grip: A Parent's Prayer at College Drop-Off

Late Summer 2016

Lord, have mercy—it's the night before we take my son to college!

This is his last night in the room that he's slept in for almost his entire 18 years.

Release me from lurking around his bedroom, but I just need to tuck him in one last time. (And release me from my urge to crawl into bed with him because that would be super-weird.)

The car is packed and the gas tank is full. Everything seems to be ready for a smooth departure tomorrow.

Release me from frantically running around the house in the morning like a crazed lunatic, looking for something I will be certain I've lost—because it'll probably just be my mind. (Right now "leaving" and "losing" feels like the same thing.)

Our parking permit is in hand, and the residence hall move-in time is confirmed.

Release me from feeling overwhelmed by the crowds and chaos of a thousand parents and students lugging around box fans and crates of bedding. (And please release the elevator from its ridiculous crawl, because I'm not walking up eight flights of stairs with a mini-fridge.)

We'll get him all moved in and unpacked.

Release me from being an over-controlling, overbearing "nester" who obsesses about storage space and knickknack placement. (But Lord, let me make his bed…I NEED TO MAKE THAT BED!)

We'll probably wander the campus a bit, maybe grab a bite to eat and stop by the bookstore.

Release me from the urge in a moment of weakness to buy any sort of cheesy bumper sticker or garments that say "MSU MOM."

And then it will be time for me to leave. Without him, because he is staying there.

> *Oh Lord, release me from the overwhelming grief I'm feeling right now and replace it with hope and excitement for his new life.*

> *Help me put one foot in front of the other and release my tears after I make it to the car so I can ugly cry on my steering wheel instead of making a scene in public.*

> *Release me from being heartbroken if I don't hear from him as often as I'd like. (And help me figure out Snapchat so I can stalk him on social media.)*

> *Release me from worrying about things beyond my control—like him falling off his loft bed, contracting meningitis, fraternity hazing, his refusal to use an umbrella, natural disasters, cult abduction, and poor choices—and remind me that despite the inevitable challenges he'll face that you're directing his path.*

> *Release my grip when I hug him one last time and I don't want to let go, and remind me I've raised a young man who's ready to spread his wings.*

> *Oh…and one more thing, Lord.*

> *Hold me tightly in your peace and comfort tomorrow as I release him to you.*

> *Even though he's always been yours.*

> *Lord, in your mercy, hear my prayer.*

Digging Deeper—Devotions and Journaling

As you anticipate the day of college drop-off, what words on your heart do you want to share with God? Journal your own prayer here.

Our love for our kids is bigger than our sadness as they leave the nest. And God's love is big enough to cover us and give us hope and peace in this painful transition.

Chapter 4

A Cup of Suffering:
Finding Hope in the
Days After Drop-Off

"…a time to mourn."

Late Summer 2016

When I hugged my son Nate goodbye at college and watched him walk into the next chapter of his life, it was hard.

Really hard.

But somehow I managed to make it back to the car, and I only ugly cried for the first 30 miles of the 10-hour car ride home.

I rallied myself by focusing my thoughts on the beautiful campus where we'd left him behind, how nice his roommate was, and how perfectly the school seemed to fit him.

I was proud and excited for him, and I kept treading in that spot to avoid sinking below the surface into the darker waters of sadness.

But when we finally pulled into our driveway around 1 a.m., I was suddenly struck with a wave of grief that was so visceral it took my breath away.

"I need to call Nate and say goodnight!" I wailed to my husband, who calmly reminded me that our son hates to talk on the phone, and that I needed to give him some space to adjust and not pester him with my needs.

I stared at my phone, desperate to hear his voice with a yearning that only a mama can understand, but I simply texted: "We just got home—heading to bed. Goodnight, buddy. I love you."

"I love you too" he texted back.

I was thrilled, and shrieked, "He's still up! Let's call him really quick—I JUST NEED TO TALK TO HIM!"

My husband shook his head and wrapped his arms around me while gently prying my phone from my hands.

"It might be what *you* need, but it's not what *he* needs right now," my husband whispered. "You can call him tomorrow, but you've got to remember that letting go is a process and your job is to keep supporting that momentum. Don't overwhelm him with your needs. Keep putting his needs before your own— that's what parents do."

And then I melted into a heap of hot mess on the floor, bemoaning this whole wretched parenting gig with all of its suffering and sacrifices, guilt and grief, "oughts" and "shoulds"—even back to the sleepless nights and stretch marks.

My husband waited patiently for my sob/rant fest to subside and then reminded me that the reason I was so sad was that I loved motherhood and was grieving my kids growing up.

"But hasn't all the pain been worth it?" he asked.

Ugh. How ironic.

Since that epic meltdown, I've continued on an emotional roller coaster that's been a combination of missing my son's daily presence and the turmoil of restraining my constant urge to contact him. *To call or not to call? To text or not to text?*

I'm longing to hear stories about the friends he's making. And if things are going well with his roommate. And if he likes the dining hall food. And his classes. And the weather. And if he's joined any clubs. And if he got his books. And if he's sleeping well. And if he misses home.

And if he misses me.

All of these mama-musings have been swirling around in my head daily, along with the urge to simply connect with him. To reach for him. To know he's there and thriving. To give me some relief from the suffocating grief of letting go.

It's what *I* need in order to process his departure from home and fill the empty space he's left behind. But it's not what *he* needs for an unencumbered entry into this new season of independence.

I remind myself of this when I start sliding into a state of despair…but it's not easy. For some reason my urge to reach out is constant and overbearing, and each time I resist the temptation I'm doused with a fresh wave of sadness that only increases my suffering in the stark awareness of his absence.

But, like so many other times I've endured sufferings along the path of life and motherhood, when my heart feels like it can't bear the burden anymore—I reach for God. (OK—more like I bolt wildly into his arms like a small hysterical child who's just fallen off her bike—but God's cool with that.)

And somehow God's presence reminds me that although love, suffering, and sacrifice are inextricably woven together, *love always wins.*

We're sad because we love our kids so much and letting them go is hard. And missing them hurts. And we feel bad (and lonely and a little crazy) for feeling sad because we can't understand how something "good" can feel so painful.

But our love is still bigger than our sadness. And God's love is big enough to cover us, to give us hope and peace in this painful transition.

Suffering and sacrifice are simply part of the journey of loving unconditionally. It's God's economy.

Jesus' life on earth is the masterpiece of this truth.

Jesus sacrificed his life out of love for us, but I often forget that he also *suffered* for us. He not only felt the slow, excruciating physical pain of crucifixion, but he also suffered the emotional pain of dreading what was to come.

In the New Testament we see this when Jesus was in the garden of Gethsemane with his disciples and he slipped aside to pray just before he was arrested.

> " 'Father, if you are willing, take this cup from me; yet not my will, but yours be done.' An angel from heaven appeared to him and strengthened him. And being in anguish, he prayed more earnestly, and his sweat was like drops of blood falling to the ground"
> Luke 22:42-44. (NIV)

The cup Jesus refers to is the cup of suffering. But his cup of suffering held much more than his own suffering. It was also filled with all the bitterness of the sins of man and the wrath of God—a cup Jesus knew he must drink in order for us to have fellowship with God. (That's a much bigger cup than I've ever had to bear!)

But what I see in Jesus' prayer is the natural suffering and pain of a genuine human being—the pain of someone who was fully man as well as fully divine. For some reason Jesus' suffering—not just his sacrifice—was required in this ultimate act of love.

Jesus understands what human suffering is all about. He's been there. He gets it, and he gets us.

I take comfort in knowing that the grief and suffering I feel as a mother during this season of letting go is a normal and natural part of loving.

I take comfort sharing my pain with a God who understands.

I take comfort in knowing that Jesus himself cried out for relief when the burden got too heavy.

And I take comfort in knowing that suffering is not the end of the story…it is simply a season. And it will pass.

Hope is around the corner, and good things are still to come.

This I know for sure.

Digging Deeper—Devotions and Journaling

Read and reflect on the following passage from the Bible:

> *"...We also glory in our sufferings, because we know that suffering produces perseverance; perseverance, character; and character, hope. And hope does not put us to shame, because God's love has been poured out into our hearts through the Holy Spirit, who has been given to us" Romans 5:3-5. (NIV)*

Share your heart with God in a time of prayer—talking to him and listening, too. Tell God about your process of letting go—sharing your struggles, needs, and fears.

Ask God: ***Lord, what do you want to teach me from this season? How can I replace my sadness with your peace and hope today?*** Journal the words the Holy Spirit brings to you below.

_____

_____

_____

_____

_____

_____

_____

_____

_____

_____

_____

_____

_____

Journal a prayer for your son or daughter as he or she heads into these new weeks of school.

_____

_____

_____

_____

_____

_____

_____

_____

_____

_____

_____

_____

_____

_____

_____

_____

_____

_____

Up for a Challenge?

Send your son or daughter a copy of this prayer by mail or email.

Losing some of my identity that was tied into the busyness and "doings" of parenthood is clearing a path toward embracing my true identity that's ironically not even really about me—it's about who I am in Christ. My identity is about whose I am.

(Not whose mom I am.)

Chapter 5

Losing Myself and Finding More of Jesus

"...a time to be born and a time to die."

Fall 2013

I was at my mailbox last weekend and saw my neighbor Beth weeding her flower bed. As I strolled over to say hello, I noticed she wasn't just weeding…

She was weeping.

On her knees. Right there on the front lawn.

I asked if she was OK, and she explained that they'd just dropped off Logan, the last of her three kids, at college the day before.

She sobbed, "I AM NOT OK—I AM TOTALLY LOST!"

She confessed that when she walked by Logan's empty bedroom last night, she realized it was the first time since the day he was born she didn't need to turn on his night light.

The night light ritual represented 18 years of mama-nurturing rhythm and at that moment, she suddenly recognized how much the routine of doing little daily mom things was over for good. She felt empty, lonely, and lost.

Apparently this realization also caused her to burst into tears, hurl herself onto his bed, and bury her face in his sheets to inhale the lingering scent of her son. *All night long.*

"His smell isn't going to last forever, and it's ALL I have left!" she wailed.

(OK—she totally lost me at lying facedown on her son's sheets to intentionally breathe in the scent of teenage boy. I personally avoid any direct contact with my teenage sons' bedding because I can smell it from the hallway…gag.)

But my conversation with Beth reminded me of my feelings of loss and bewilderment about my identity when my daughter, Paige, left for college. I spent a lot of time wondering about what her leaving for college meant for me.

Being a mother is the lens through which I usually see my existence. Even though I've had a rewarding professional career, being a mother is the most important job I've ever had.

Being a mother is who I am.

Or so I've thought.

Perhaps being a mother is an identity that swallowed me whole.

Amid all of the sacrifice and busyness of being a mom and the satisfaction of feeling valuable, I've started to recognize that being a mother is NOT all that I am. But being a mother has been God's way of letting me know something even more important about myself…and about him.

You see, when I held my daughter right after she was born, I finally experienced what unconditional love felt like. My first epiphany as a parent was finally being able to comprehend how much God really loves us. Another mom described it so well: "God gave me a baby girl so that I can truly understand how he feels about *his* baby girl."

And watching Paige walk up the steps of her freshman dorm as our car drove away brought part 2 of the epiphany: That deep, anguished, lie-facedown-on-their-sheets-longing to hold our babies close and stay connected in their lives even though we're releasing them to be independent is exactly how our heavenly Father yearns for us.

Because we are *all* beloved children of the King.

Before we were mothers, or fathers, or grandparents—before we ever accomplished anything in our lives with our *doing*—we were known, valued, and loved simply for our *being*.

The promise of the gospel is all the proof we'll ever need.

And how often I forget that.

I forget as I independently march through life measuring my worth by worldly standards and determined to control the destiny of myself and my loved ones through my own endeavors.

The journey of parenthood will never be over. The seasons of *doing* will wane as our kids grow up, but we'll never stop *being* their parents.

Someday just *being* is going to be enough.

I'm learning to rest more in the *being* of my life. Losing some of my identity tied into the busyness and "doings" of parenthood is clearing a path toward embracing my true identity about who I am in Christ.

That identity is about whose I am…not whose mom I am.

Digging Deeper—Devotions and Journaling

Go sit quietly in your son or daughter's bedroom and look around. (Sniff the sheets if you dare!)

Let your mind wander for a few minutes through a mental collage of sacred lifetime moments with your child—from the day they were born, to watching them take their first steps, to watching them walk away at college.

Do you feel that overwhelming sense of pride and love mixed with a raw, deep longing in your heart? Consider this feeling an invitation—an outstretched hand from your heavenly Father beckoning you into his loving embrace. Come to him, and rest in the newfound understanding of how God feels about you and how he desires a connected relationship with his precious child every single day.

Rest in Jesus now—as you sit surrounded by reminders of your child. You're not alone.

Read and reflect on the following passage from the Bible:

"You made all the delicate, inner parts of my body and knit me together in my mother's womb. Thank you for making me so wonderfully complex! Your workmanship is marvelous—how well I know it. You watched me as I was being formed in utter seclusion, as I was woven together in the dark of the womb. You saw me before I was born. Every day of my life was recorded in your book. Every moment was laid out before a single day had passed. How precious are your thoughts about me, O God. They cannot be numbered!" Psalm 139:13-17. (NLT)

Read this passage again. And again. Let your heart absorb these words spoken directly to you from your heavenly Father.

Find a quiet place where you can share your heart with God in a time of prayer. Talk with him, and listen, too. Ask Jesus: *Who do you say that I am?*

Journal the words the Holy Spirit brings to you below.

_____

_____

_____

_____

_____

_____

_____

Think about the titles you wear and the roles you fill and how much they influence your identity. Whether it's the role of parent, or spouse, or perhaps your job title, what are they? List them below—as many as you can think of—and then read on when you've finished.

_____

_____

_____

_____

_____

_____

_____

_____

_____

You've listed how you're known—to others and to yourself. Earlier you asked Jesus who *he* says you are and listened for what he said.

A question: As you compare the two lists—who Jesus says you are and who others (and perhaps you yourself) say you are—how do the two lists compare? And is there anything in the second list that gets in the way of your fully embracing what's in the first? If so, draw a line through that item on your second list.

Anything you drew a line through? That's something for you and Jesus to talk more about.

> *"Since you have been raised to new life with Christ, set your sights on the realities of heaven, where Christ sits in the place of honor at God's right hand. Think about the things of heaven, not the things of earth. For you died to this life, and your real life is hidden with Christ in God"* Colossians 3:1-3. (NLT)

Up for a Challenge?

Launch a fearless conversation with your college-age loved one about *their* true identity.

Young adulthood is a key time of self-discovery as our kids wrestle with the question, "Who am I, REALLY?" It's also an important topic of conversation for parents and their college-age kids, as it offers significant insights into how young adults view themselves and their value.

Invite your son or daughter to talk about what they've discovered about their identity since entering college. Enter into the conversation with the intent to truly listen with an open mind.

A non-threatening way to do this is simply by asking open-ended questions such as:

- What things about yourself have surprised you the most since you got to college?

- What are two important traits you've learned about yourself since you left home?

- Is there a place/group of people you've found on campus where you feel most comfortable and accepted? Tell me about it.

- How has your faith impacted your view of yourself?

- Who do you think Jesus says that you are? In what ways is this important to your identity—or isn't it?

Listen first. Let them speak as much—or as little—as they want to. Resist the urge to correct or rebut what they're saying. Instead, follow up with questions such as "Why is that?" or "Why might you feel this way?"

If asked about your experience, or if you feel it's your turn to share, be transparent and honest about your discoveries about how your identity has been challenged during times of transition—including now. Explaining what you're doing (or what you'd like to be doing) to deepen your relationship with Jesus in the midst of this transition is a great way to have a mature, meaningful faith conversation about identity in Christ.

Remind your son or daughter that they're loved—by you and by God. They're never too old to hear it! And if you're comfortable, end your conversation by praying together.

Part 2:
Learning to Fly

"But those who hope in the Lord will renew their strength. They will soar on wings like eagles; they will run and not grow weary, they will walk and not be faint" Isaiah 40:31. (NIV)

Perhaps freedom doesn't come from escaping something that's controlling us. Perhaps it comes from releasing our grip on what we're trying to control and surrendering to something greater.

Chapter 6

Discovering the Truth About Freedom

"...a time to dance."

Fall 2013

When my kids were little, my parents would occasionally host a grandkids sleepover night so my husband and I could enjoy the freedom of a date night that actually extended through the night and into a glorious morning of sleeping in without the intrusion of little people.

I used to count down the days to this brief encounter with "freedom," but then inevitably something would happen that robbed me of the peace of truly enjoying it.

From croupy coughs to spiking fevers, there was always something nagging inside my mama-brain that made it impossible for me to let go and relax for those 24 hours of freedom. I felt guilty for not being there. I HAD to check in. I HAD to make sure everything was OK.

Because for me, freedom came from the peace of mind that only seemed achievable when I had the ability to keep everything under control.

Fast forward through elementary, middle school, and high school. There was finally freedom from diapers, babysitters, and, eventually, even from carpools. Gone were the days when my time was demanded every waking moment. My teenagers were so absorbed in their busy lives that I became the one following them around the house begging for a few minutes of attention.

But while freedom from so many of the demands of parenting young children was evident, I was still a slave to the fear of not being in control.

The more independent my kids became, the more I struggled with worry. I carried the weight of worrying and wondering about them and feeling clueless about what was really going on in their lives. I was confident in the great kids I'd been blessed with, but I couldn't shake the ever-present paranoia that comes with raising teenagers in today's world.

And when Paige left for college, and I was the last parent to leave the residence hall on drop-off day because I was still "nesting" and decorating her dorm room at 9 p.m., I finally realized I had some reckoning to do with my soul.

I came face to face with the truth that I don't do the "letting go" thing very well.

Not at all.

And because God always seems to show up in crazy-cool ways when we start paying attention to what's stirring in our soul, the topic of my Bible study a few days after college drop-off was "freedom."

"What does freedom mean to you?" was a question we discussed.

We all talked of freedom from things like obligations, from debt, from illness, from emotional heartache, from addiction, from fear, from anxiety, from ties to unhealthy relationships. *All stuff real life is made of.*

The more we talked, the more it dawned on me that we often define *freedom* as escaping from the binds of something that we feel has gripped our life.

Then there was the next question: "Where have you felt freedom lately?"

And we shared things like "having lunch with a dear friend and we just laughed and laughed," "taking my dog for a leisurely walk on a beautiful fall day," and "turning off my alarm and sleeping in last Saturday." *All stuff real life is made of.*

Despite the tough stuff enslaving our lives, freedom wasn't always absent. It showed up in laughter, in paying attention to the simple beauty of creation, in loving relationships, and in letting go.

And wherever freedom seemed to be most evident, so did the presence of God.

Perhaps freedom doesn't come from escaping something that's controlling us. Perhaps it comes from releasing our grip on what we're trying to control and surrendering to something greater.

Perhaps it's not about moving *away* from but closer *toward* something else.

Perhaps that "something" is Jesus.

Digging Deeper—Devotions and Journaling

As kids leave the nest, this new season ushers in a sense of freedom in new ways for families. For our young adult kids, they're experiencing what it's like to control their routine and make more choices. For parents, this freedom might feel like a release from some of our kids' former daily activities that once dominated our schedule: sporting events to attend, dinners to make, and a continuous flow of never-ending laundry.

But on the flip side, with this new freedom our kids discover there's a price: facing tough decisions solo, experiencing consequences, and coping with the pressure to succeed. For parents, though our homes might be cleaner and quieter, the lack of daily visibility into our kids' lives often means our thoughts are consumed with wondering or worrying about them. And the costs of college can become a financial burden for both kids and parents—managing the expenses and debt can feel like a never-ending process.

Find a quiet place where you can relax and listen to what Jesus has to say to you about this: **How are you experiencing freedom in this new season of your life?**

As you consider freedom, read and reflect on the following verses from the Bible:

"Then you will know the truth, and the truth will set you free" John 8:32. (NIV)

"Jesus answered, "I am the way and the truth and the life. No one comes to the Father except through me" John 14:6. (NIV)

Journal your thoughts about this question, listening for what Jesus might have to say: **What does freedom mean to you?**

Freedom is one thing; finding ourselves enslaved is another. Read and reflect on the following verses from the Bible:

> *"The temptations in your life are no different from what others experience. And God is faithful. He will not allow the temptation to be more than you can stand. When you are tempted, he will show you a way out so that you can endure"* 1 Corinthians 10:13. (NLT)

> *"So Christ has truly set us free. Now make sure that you stay free, and don't get tied up again in slavery to the law"* Galatians 5:1. (NLT)

Journal your thoughts about this question: **What things in your life are making you feel enslaved?**

_____

_____

_____

_____

_____

_____

_____

_____

_____

_____

_____

_____

_____

Freedom—you can feel it. But where are you feeling it? Read and reflect on this verse from the Bible:

"For the Lord is the Spirit, and wherever the Spirit of the Lord is, there is freedom" 2 Corinthians 3:17. (NLT)

Now journal your thoughts about this question: **When and where have you felt the most freedom in your life recently?**

Up for a Challenge?

Ponder what you've written about freedom in your life and where you are most aware of God's presence. *In the areas where you feel enslaved, how might surrendering those things to Jesus impact your sense of freedom and bring you the peace he promises?*

Share your heart with Jesus. Compose a prayer below, asking him to bring peace to those areas of your life that are keeping you from experiencing freedom and life in him.

I've learned
that for both my
son and me,
surviving
and thriving
in this season of
"letting go"
simply means
"letting God."

Chapter 7

Phoning Home: Parenting After the Glitter of College Wears Off

"…a time to be silent and a time to speak."

Early Fall 2016

Not too long ago, I finally got "the text" from my college freshman son.

It had been three weeks since college drop-off day, and I'd worked hard not to pester him too much with my needy texts, phone calls, and questions. Every so often I'd text him a quick "love and miss you" along with a pertinent question I'd been dying to have answered, like if he's happy, if he's making friends, if he's liking class, and so on.

Consistently his responses back to my texts have been super-short: "It's great!!" "Yes!!" "Love you too!!"

I've only talked to him on a handful of occasions. Every time I call he seems to be hurrying to class or hanging out with friends.

As a mom who struggles with the process of letting go, being so disconnected from his new life has been tough. He's always been an independent kid, but my only assurances that he was doing OK were a plethora of exclamation points in his brief but upbeat text responses.

Until I got a text from him that began with "UGH."

The full text was practically a novel—a venting of frustration about how hard his calculus class was, how he'd never struggled with math until now, how he was worried a bad grade would cause him to lose his scholarship, how his demanding class schedule conflicted with club baseball practice and he realized he couldn't do both, and how stressed and confused he was about what he really wanted to do for a career.

It ended with, "I think I want to change my major. Please don't be mad. Can we talk?"

And in that moment, this mama felt the heavens part with rays of light and an angels' chorus singing "Hallelujah!"

My role as his mother—as a sounding board, advisor, and encourager—was not over. He was reaching out for wisdom and guidance because he was finally ready for it.

And I was ready for it, too.

I'm not a stranger to receiving this kind of text at approximately the three- to four-week mark of freshman or sophomore year of college. My daughter, Paige, now a college senior, had also reached out around this time as the glitter of her freshman year wore off, revealing the reality of classes, pressure, and uncertainty underneath.

And in just the last week, four of my friends who have kids in college mentioned getting a similar phone call recently. Homesickness. Frustration. Roommate tension. Uncertainties about the direction of their major. Lack of money.

'Tis the season of reality—of our college-age kids discovering that the freedom that comes from independence also comes with the gravity of responsibility. Our once-confident kids who breezed through high school with the attitude of "I can be anything when I grow up" now realize that choosing a career path is not like picking out a Halloween costume. College isn't like summer camp. This thing called "adulting" is so much more than an age on a driver's license.

For my son, his sudden epiphany that he wanted to be a policeman instead of a doctor meant navigating the university's complicated system of changing his major from health sciences/pre-med to sociology/criminology. He had to get a new academic advisor. Some of his hardest first semester classes were now empty credit hours. It was too late to switch classes, so he'd have to catch up with his new plan next semester. He might have to take summer classes, and he might not even be able to get his degree in four years.

As he poured out all of these details to me on the phone, I listened. Occasionally I asked a few questions to explore what was underneath the surface, but mostly I just listened. And the more I listened, the more he talked. And vented. And shared.

Finally, he got exasperated and said, "Mom! What do you think I should do? TELL ME WHAT YOU THINK I SHOULD DO!"

"I think you should slow down, take a deep breath, and keep exploring the answer, buddy," I told him.

Boom! Motherhood clearly isn't over, but the heartwrenching process of letting go and accepting the change in his life is also changing me.

I've been grieving the loss of my old role as the mother of a boy, and in the process I'm beginning to embrace my new role as the mother of a young man.

This is a new season of parenthood in which my most important contribution doesn't mean having the right answers. My job description as a mom no longer consists of directing, correcting, and protecting. It has evolved into coaching and encouraging him along the path of exploring, evaluating, and making decisions that he can own himself.

And the person I need to keep pointing him to as he faces these big life choices is not me, it's God. That is the greatest contribution that I can give him as his mother.

As much as I wanted to insert a directive opinion and calm his frantic rant with helpful solutions, I simply encouraged him to be open. I reminded him that God created him for a purpose and has a plan for him, and I told him he should seek God's peace and guidance in prayer and a lot of listening. I reminded him that he's only 18 years old, and his path to his future career will probably have several hairpin turns along the way.

I reminded him that he's not alone, that God is with him every step. And I reminded him that I loved him no matter what and would support any decision he made as long as he felt it was God's direction.

Parenting young adult kids brings a truth to light that I can see more clearly now: *Parenthood is a lifelong collaboration with God.*

God has always been alongside us, but when our kids are small and needy it sometimes feels as if we're the only people in the game. Now that my son has left home, I realize that God's role in his life will become more apparent as my role naturally steps back.

Since our conversation, my texts to my son have changed in tone to reflect a shift that's happened in my heart. Although I still miss him, I'm no longer reaching out as the desperately sad mom who's worried about intruding on his new independence but still dying to know the mundane details of his life.

I now text him whenever I feel the urge, offering a short Bible verse or simple reminder that I'm praying for him, that I believe in him, and that I love him. I am his advocate, listener, and encourager.

I've got on a new mom-skin that I'm wearing with confidence.

I've realized my son still values and trusts my role as his mother. I know he loves me and he knows I love him. I know he's doing OK but also facing the normal challenges and realities of college. I know he'll feel the weight of some burdens, but instead of over-worrying or taking them on for him, I'll point him to the One who has asked to carry them.

And I know he'll reach out if he needs me—and I'll always be there. But I'm comfortable inviting God to be his go-to person.

I've reclaimed an appropriate place in his life, and it finally feels right.

And I've learned that for both my son and me, surviving and thriving in this season of "letting go" simply means "letting God."

Digging Deeper—Devotions and Journaling

Read and reflect on the following verse from the Bible:

> *"He must increase, but I must decrease"* John
> 3:30. *(KJV)*

With that passage in mind, consider this: Is God nudging you to hand over the reins somewhere in your life? In the lives of your family members?

Ask God: ***Lord, where do I need more of you and less of me?***

Journal the words the Holy Spirit brings to you below.

_____

_____

_____

_____

_____

_____

_____

_____

_____

Now read and reflect on the following verse from the Bible:

> *"So be strong and courageous! Do not be afraid and*
> *do not panic before them. For the Lord your God will*
> *personally go ahead of you. He will neither fail you*
> *nor abandon you"* Deuteronomy 31:6. *(NLT)*

Keeping this verse in mind, share this prayer with God, listening for his response:

> *Lord, ease my fear and guide my way as I continue to lead my kids to you. Draw them to you, reveal your comforting presence to them, and walk beside them along their path to the future you have planned for them.*

Write your own prayer for your college student, mentioning what they're facing now and considering their future. Share your heart, hopes, and dreams for them.

_____

_____

_____

_____

_____

_____

_____

_____

_____

_____

_____

Up for a Challenge?

Send your son or daughter a copy of the prayer you wrote by mail or email.

No matter how
old they get,
**we'll never
stop missing
our kids.**

And they'll never
stop needing to
be reminded of how
deeply they
are loved.

Chapter 8

Parenthood Is Never Over, and Love Never Ends

"...a time to love"

Late Fall 2016

Ever since I left for college I've always lived more than a thousand miles away from home.

Starting when I was a freshman, my mom and dad created a tradition of visiting every year mid-fall for a weekend and taking me and all of my college friends out for fancy meals.

My parents have kept up their annual fall visits to see me and my family, and in their retirement they've extended their time by renting a nearby cabin in the mountains of Colorado for a month. They enjoy hiking during the week and pop in for a visit on the weekends when we're not busy. It's the low-key, casual way we've been visiting together for years.

When my son Nate chose to attend college in Montana, my parents were thrilled to add a trip to Bozeman to their western states fall hiking tour. They hoped to tag along on a parents' weekend with me recently to visit him. We'd planned for a mid-October trip, but my schedule got crazy-busy, and Nate seemed quite fine with the reality that a visit wasn't going to pan out.

Despite *his* obvious contentment to be left alone, I missed my son terribly and I felt so guilty for not making a parental appearance his first semester. I wondered if his detached attitude meant that I *should* make visiting more of a priority and if I was internalizing his detachment as rejection and therefore subconsciously avoiding a visit.

I thought back to times in college my mom and dad had visited me. I loved seeing them, introducing them to my friends, and especially eating nice restaurant food. But despite my appreciation and enjoyment of time with my parents, I was never devastated about saying goodbye when they left. I loved them very much, but I also loved my independence and the fact that my mom had often reminded me "I've raised you to survive in a world without me."

My mom's survival mantra and her steady nudging of me to lean on God instead of on her is something I've always derived strength and confidence from. With that in mind, I decided my non-visit strategy was the best thing for my son, even though my parents announced they were still heading up to see him for a college visit no matter what anyone thought.

It was perfect! I was relieved that the grandparents could be my "mole" and sniff out how Nate was doing and give me the scoop on his whole college scene. They would be spending three days there, which gave them plenty of time to explore the area and get a sense of how things were going. I called them on their drive up to review the plan of everything I needed them to report back to me.

During their visit in Montana, I proceeded to call my parents several times every day to get an update. Sometimes they were too busy to answer the phone, responding with a brief text to let me know everything was fine.

Because I wanted more than a quick text of reassurance, I persisted with the phone calls until they responded with a return phone call. I felt desperately disconnected from my son, and I needed to know all of the details about how he was doing.

On the final night of their visit in Montana, my mom answered the phone and said, "You've called me more in the last three days than you have in the last five years...but I like it!"

There was something in her voice that caught my attention. It was a yearning that my heart keenly picked up on since I was also in the same place of longing to hear from my own child.

Once again I thought back to my own college days. We didn't have cellphones then, and long-distance calls were expensive so we didn't talk often. Our communication was primarily via mail—real mail—which meant my mom frequently sent me letters and care packages, and I occasionally remembered to thank her.

After sophomore year when I stopped coming home for college breaks and rebelliously headed out to Colorado to be with a cowboy I'd gotten engaged to, the mail stopped and our communication dwindled to a rare phone call every few months. And for the past two decades this has been the norm of our verbal communication.

Fortunately, my parents have adapted to texting, and this has increased our connection to communicating much more frequently—but we don't really talk much. As they've aged, I've subtly sensed their need for more consistent phone conversations, but since they're healthy and vibrant, I've not really paid much attention to their hints.

Until now.

The next day as my parents made the drive home from Montana, I received this text from my mom—I can only imagine how long it took her to peck all of these words out on her phone.

Dear Kami,

I have some good news and bad news. The good news is that Nate is adjusting to college and seems to be doing very well. He is studying hard, making friends, exercising, and is involved in extracurricular activities, including spiritual ones. You have done a good job of raising him. He is a responsible, fine young man.

The bad news is that because of his solid background and good fit at this wonderful school, he is not constantly thinking of you and home. He doesn't have the need to talk to his mom all the time or get her constant hugs and love. He is not longing to hear your voice. He probably won't call you often. But that isn't because he doesn't care or love you, but because he has a solid foundation to take off from. Knowing you and God are there for him allows him to move into adulthood as a strong, godly young man.

If you ever get lonely, please call your mommy. Don't forget that she still misses you, too.

Love you,

Mom

When I got her text, I wept.

I wept the tears of a fellow parent who understands the primal longing for more connection to her child.

I wept in the recognition of how a mother will always miss her baby—despite independence and distance and the years in between.

I wept because I saw how a parent was able to fulfill her role and take care of the needs of her child long after she'd grown up and in ways I'd never imagined would still matter so much.

I wept because I witnessed the powerful legacy of independence, strength, and trust in God that a mother can pass along through generations.

I wept because of the sheer irony of it all: the continuous circle of life, love, and the painful release of a grip I realized will never fully end.

I wept because this was all beautiful and true and holy beyond words.

And I wept because this was *my* mother…and I didn't realize how much she still missed me.

And I didn't realize how much I still needed to hear it.

We raise our children to have wings and to thrive on their own as independent, responsible, healthy adults. And there is a deep sense of pride in knowing we've done our job well.

But no matter how old they get, we'll never stop missing our kids.

And they'll never stop needing to be reminded of how deeply they are loved.

Digging Deeper—Devotions and Journaling

Love is a funny thing. Unlike other human emotions, true love doesn't fade with time or distance. We can even love people long after they are gone from this earth.

But when our loved ones are not in our daily lives, we miss them and it hurts. Our heart longs for them and the container of a relationship in which we are able to give and receive love.

Read and reflect on the following passage from the Bible:

> "And I am convinced that nothing can ever separate us from God's love. Neither death nor life, neither angels nor demons, neither our fears for today nor our worries about tomorrow—not even the powers of hell can separate us from God's love. No power in the sky above or in the earth below—indeed, nothing in all creation will ever be able to separate us from the love of God that is revealed in Christ Jesus our Lord" Romans 8:38-39. (NLT)

When we read God's Word and reflect on his love for us, it comforts us to be reminded of his immense love for us. Even though we *know* he loves us, we sometimes wander away from this truth and begin to wonder if he is still here—if he still loves us as fully.

Keeping in mind the verses above, share this prayer with God, listening for his response:

> Lord, envelop me in your spirit today so that I have no doubts about your presence in my life and love for me. Draw me into your embrace, and allow me to rest in your comfort as your child. Give my heart words of love from you that I need to hear.

Journal the words or thoughts that God brings to you in this loving embrace.

_____

_____

_____

_____

_____

_____

_____

_____

_____

_____

_____

_____

_____

Up for a Challenge?

There's probably someone in your life who could use a reminder of how much they are loved by you and God. Perhaps it is a child, a parent, a spouse, or another significant person in your life. Ask God to reveal who needs a loving word from you, and reach out to them. Put your words in writing if possible so they can keep them. You never know how much your words might be needed to be heard today by someone you love.

Gratitude often comes
in hindsight, when kids
look back on the
college years and
opportunities
they were given with
the grateful
perspective
that comes from
maturity.

Chapter 9

Wanted: Gratitude Without Strings Attached

"...a time to plant and a time to harvest."

Fall 2014

"Thank you for everything you do for me. I love you. I'm so blessed that you're my mom."

Those were the words texted to me by my daughter, Paige, during her sophomore year in college.

My heart swelled with love and gratitude that she was growing up to be such a wonderful, considerate young woman, reaching out to offer her mama some genuine love.

The feeling lasted for a few moments as I reread this cherished text over and over. But then something caught my attention. She had used the word *blessed.*

Hmm.

Blessed is not a normal word in her vocabulary. Although she has a vibrant, ever-growing faith and relationship with Jesus, this kid is simply not one to toss *blessed* into a random text without a motive. Something was up, and I needed to get to the bottom of it.

"Thanks for the affirmation! Is everything OK?" I responded.

"Everything is great! I love my internship with the elephant rescue project. And they've invited me to serve in Thailand for three weeks this summer!" she replied.

"How awesome! An all-expenses-paid trip to Thailand, I assume!" I texted back, knowing full well what was coming next.

"Well, they're a nonprofit, so we'd have to pay the fee and stuff…"

And two minutes later my phone rang. It was Paige, calling to explain the "fee and stuff." It was "only like" $3,750 plus the cost of airfare, of course.

I asked how she was planning to earn enough money to cover the trip since I had no intention of funding more of my daughter's international travel aspirations, and we had already committed to help fund a study-abroad experience for the second semester of her junior year.

But now her hopeful request for us to pay for a summer trip to Thailand finally sent me over the edge of sanity.

My entire annual salary is consumed by tuition and room and board, despite some merit scholarships she earned. We'd already used our savings to put our two oldest kids through college, and we still have two in high school.

Did my kids even have a clue?

They say they're grateful, and they've thanked us dutifully when I've forwarded them the receipt each time I pay a tuition bill, cellphone bill, and car insurance premium. BUT WHY IN THE WORLD DO THEY KEEP EXPECTING MORE?

Why can't I just get a text from my daughter that says she's thankful and blessed without it being a precursor to a request? How had I failed so miserably as a parent and raised such entitled kids?

Agitated, I reflected on why this ungratefulness bothered me so deeply. Was it because I had invested and sacrificed so much out of love for them?

Or was it because I needed the validation that I was a great mom and it felt nice when my kids thanked me?

My answer was a bit of both along with the following fresh perspective: I do things for my children because I love them and believe in them, and I've chosen to invest in their college education because my parents did the same for me, just as their parents did for them.

Perhaps what I view as ungratefulness is actually my kids simply trusting that I'll take care of them.

And isn't this what Jesus does for us?

God sent his one and only Son to die a hideous death as a common criminal even though he was without sin in order to give us eternal life—just because he loves us.

But there are many days I forget to live a life that oozes gratitude for this great sacrifice.

And there are many other days when I feel lonely and inadequate and I forget how much Jesus loves and wants me.

Just like my children expect that I'll take care of their dreams and aspirations, I expect God to take care of me, answer my prayers, and come through no matter what. (And I also still whine when his plans for my life don't seem to match mine.)

Yet despite my frequent lack of gratitude, he sticks with me and promises to never leave or turn his back on me.

Because his love doesn't hinge on my thanks.

I'm challenging myself to take the same attitude with my children and recognize that they really are grateful—they just don't always show it the way I'd like to see it.

Gratitude often comes in hindsight, when kids look back on the college years and opportunities they were given with the grateful perspective that comes from maturity.

And even though I'd love my children to act more thankful and text "Thank you, Mom," without any strings attached, I can't gauge my value based on the gratitude I receive in the current moment.

If I do, I'll miss the joy that comes from just being their mom and loving them unconditionally.

By the way, Paige did end up calling me out of the blue a few weeks after the sketchy "blessed" text. Her voice cracked on the other end of the phone as she apologized for her request for us to fund her Thailand trip, and she thanked me for all the ways I had sacrificed for her. No strings attached. She just wanted me to know that she really understood how blessed she was—and that she was genuinely grateful.

You're welcome, Daughter. I love you, too.

Digging Deeper—Devotions and Journaling

As our kids grow up, so do their expenses. Unfortunately, it seems as if their gratitude doesn't keep up with the pace of growth. It's easy to start feeling bitter when the bills are mounting, the stress is increasing, and the requests and expectations keep coming.

Read and reflect on the following verse from the Bible:

"Give thanks in all circumstances; for this is God's will for you in Christ Jesus" 1 Thessalonians 5:18. (NIV)

Journal your thoughts about this: **Have your kids ever appeared ungrateful for what you do for them? If so, when? How did that feel?**

Read and reflect on this Bible passage, too:

"But God is so rich in mercy, and he loved us so much,
that even though we were dead because of our sins,
he gave us life when he raised Christ from the dead.
(It is only by God's grace that you have been saved!)
For he raised us from the dead along with Christ and
seated us with him in the heavenly realms because
we are united with Christ Jesus. So God can point
to us in all future ages as examples of the incredible
wealth of his grace and kindness toward us, as shown
in all he has done for us who are united with Christ
Jesus. God saved you by his grace when you believed.
And you can't take credit for this; it is a gift from God.
Salvation is not a reward for the good things we have
done, so none of us can boast about it. For we are
God's masterpiece. He has created us anew in Christ
Jesus, so we can do the good things he planned for us
long ago" Ephesians 2:4-10. (NLT)

Journal your thoughts about this: **Yes, Jesus saved you from**
your sin. But he didn't just save you from—he also saved you to.
To become the person you can become. To do what he calls you
to do. So rather than thinking only about what he saved you
from, focus on this: What did he save you to?

_____

_____

_____

_____

_____

_____

Finally, read and reflect on this passage from the Bible:

"And now, just as you accepted Christ Jesus as your Lord, you must continue to follow him. Let your roots grow down into him, and let your lives be built on him. Then your faith will grow strong in the truth you were taught, and you will overflow with thankfulness" Colossians 2:6-7. (NLT)

Reflect on moments in your life when you felt an overflowing gratitude for your relationship with Jesus. What prompted those moments? What might you do to experience more of those moments? Journal your thoughts below.

_____

_____

_____

_____

_____

_____

_____

_____

_____

_____

_____

_____

_____

We had officially entered
into a new season
that consisted of a rhythm
of coming and going,
where each goodbye would
further cement the truth
that "home"
was no longer where
she resided, but where
she came to visit.

Chapter 10

What to Expect (Realistically) When Your Kid Comes Home on College Break

"…a time to scatter stones and a time to gather them."

Fall 2004 & 2013

"I'm so excited that Zach finally comes home today!" said Zach's mom when I ran into her in the grocery store the day before Thanksgiving back in 2004.

Her face was glowing with joy at the anticipation of Zach's pending homecoming. Zach was a football player at a college almost a thousand miles away, and she hadn't seen him since dropping him off in July for summer training.

Zach was the best friend of my stepson, Chris, and it was their freshman year of college. Chris was attending college locally, so our transition with him hadn't been too tough. But the scattering of his friends to various colleges across the country had left an odd emptiness in our home that was hard to get used to.

Our house had always been the place where Chris' friends gathered, often camping out on our basement couch for days. I missed the constant coming and going of these big, sweet high school boys who I loved like my own, their noisy chaos and the giant pairs of sneakers that had always cluttered the front hallway. My three biological kids were still in elementary school, but I'd cherished the privilege of getting to "taste-test" parenthood during the high school and young adult years as Chris' stepmom.

As that Thanksgiving approached, I looked forward to our home being full again with Chris and his friends. When they started showing up a few days before Thanksgiving to reunite, I welcomed them all with open arms.

It never occurred to me that Zach had told his mom he wasn't coming home until Wednesday. But as I saw her excitement about finally being able to see her son, I realized she didn't know he'd actually been sleeping on our couch for the past two nights.

I told her to give him a hug from me and quickly bolted from the grocery store to confront my basement full of freshman stowaways.

"Everybody out! It's time to go home to your families! NOW!" I announced. Pulling Zach aside, I hissed, "I ran into your mom at the grocery store this morning—apparently she had no clue that you're already in town!"

"You didn't tell her, did you?" asked Zach, clearly terrified. "I just wanted to spend time with my friends, and I know once I go home she's not going to let me leave."

Fortunately, I hadn't told her—I didn't have the heart to break *her* heart with that news. And I could understand Zach's dilemma of wanting to see his friends but not disappoint his parents.

Nearly a decade later when I anticipated my daughter Paige's arrival home for Thanksgiving and Christmas break of her freshman year, I couldn't stop thinking about the scenario with Zach.

I tried to put a reality check on my expectations for her return from college, abandoning my hopeful vision of spending every possible minute together as a family. I didn't want my heart to be shattered with disappointment or drive her to have to lie about her whereabouts.

I knew she'd want to spend time with her friends, and sharing what little time we had wasn't easy. But at least I'd been prepared for what to expect.

Or so I thought.

I'd been prepared for her arrival home, looking forward to savoring our time together but respecting the balance of time for friends and family. I'd accepted that she missed her friends more than her mom—it was just the reality of how most college freshmen feel.

But what I *hadn't* expected was that by the end of Christmas break it would be so painfully obvious she was ready to go back to college and reclaim her independence.

She grew antsy and somewhat irritable as her time at home drew to a close. I tried to rationalize her attitude as a subconscious coping mechanism that young adult kids must use to process the separation. But when she said "I miss my bed," referring to her crappy dorm bed that consisted of a 5-inch-thick piece of vinyl, I knew our time together was up.

It was time to say goodbye. *Again.*

We had officially entered into a new season that consisted of a rhythm of coming and going, where each goodbye would further cement the truth that "home" was no longer where she resided, but where she came to visit.

She'd left the nest, and I should have expected that now her wings required space to fly.

Since experiencing phase 2 of letting go after Paige's first Christmas home from college, I've adjusted my expectations and learned to embrace the goodness of this reality.

It's bittersweet.

I think it will *always* be bittersweet.

Digging Deeper—Devotions and Journaling

Have you ever had a picture in your head of how things are "supposed" to be, only to be disappointed when they didn't turn out like you imagined they would?

It's easy to let our hopes for how we want things to turn out become our expectations. And when circumstances don't meet our expectations, we get disappointed, hurt, or frustrated.

Sometimes we have expectations about small things—such as how events of our day should go. And sometimes we have expectations about big things—life things—like our career, our kids' futures, and our relationships.

God's plans don't always look like our plans, but we can be assured he does have a plan for us.

Read and reflect on the following passages from the Bible:

"My soul, wait silently for God alone, for my expectation is from Him" Psalm 62:5. (NKJV)

"And we know that God causes everything to work together for the good of those who love God and are called according to his purpose for them" Romans 8:28. (NLT)

What visions of how your life is "supposed to be" are preventing you from the true peace that comes with accepting God's plans? Journal your thoughts below.

Up for a Challenge?

As you look forward to the return of your college student for holiday breaks, what expectations are on your mind? In what ways might you prepare for their return that will prevent conflict or disappointment? Are there certain expectations you need to communicate in advance such as specific times to gather with family, house rules or curfews, and so on?

Write a list of topics and expectations to discuss, and invite your college student's input in the process.

We don't earn the right for God's help based on the severity of our needs.

We don't **earn the right** for God's presence. Period.

Because we don't need to.

We have Jesus, and **we have grace.** And they're gifts.

Chapter 11

Chasing Peace in the Chaos

"...a time for peace."

Winter 2015

It was a chilly December morning and I was mentally processing my to-do list during my morning drive to work. It included the usual rundown of the day's meetings and project deadlines, but there was also much more than what appeared on my Outlook calendar.

I could feel my anxiety mounting as I remembered the other 67,000 things it felt like I needed to accomplish before noon:

- Stop at the post office to overnight to my nieces and nephews the gifts that have been sitting in my car for two weeks. (WHY do I always spend more in overnight postage than the actual costs of the gifts—EVERY. SINGLE. YEAR?)

- Contact our insurance company about a claim denial involving our youngest son (who had just gotten his driver's permit) and his recent car-versus-garage-door incident.

- Contact the yearbook ad people to beg for any remaining senior year farewell ad spots because I'd missed the December 1st deadline.

- Beg for an appointment with the dog groomer before we have 12 relatives visiting this week for Christmas. (Oh no. I forgot to order the 26-pound organic, fresh, free-range turkey that my in-laws mentioned. I think I was supposed to do that weeks ago…)

My heart was pounding beyond the effects of the quadruple venti soy mocha from Starbucks I was sipping, and I started to feel lightheaded.

I pulled my car to the side of the road, closed my eyes, breathed deeply, and reached out to God for help.

Within an instant, I was awash with guilt.

My mind flashed to everything in the news recently—the bombings, the shootings, the never-ending plight of refugees.

There were certainly people with much bigger problems than mine. What right did I have to be bothering God with my shallow pleas because I was struggling with First World problems like a busy schedule?

I'm no stranger to tough times, and I've had some legitimate drop-to-my knees moments when all I could cling to was God. Like when my first marriage crumbled and I was suddenly a single mom with three kids under age 6. Like when the doctor spotted what he believed was osteosarcoma (bone cancer) on my son's X-ray that thankfully turned out to be benign.

In light of this, I felt paralyzed with confusion. Was it OK to feel desperate before God on a basically good day for something as benign as busyness? Shouldn't I be more reverent and grateful that things aren't that bad?

And then I opened my eyes and saw the answer to my question.

On this blustery winter morning, with the ominous dark skies of a storm rolling in over the mountains, the sun had peeked out and there was a brilliant rainbow stretching across the landscape in front of my car.

A rainbow. In December. So weird!

And then—not even kidding—I saw the bright white reflection of a flock of seagulls rising against a dark sky, swirling in front of the rainbow.

Seagulls. In COLORADO.

(OK, so it would have been cooler if they had been white doves. And the seagulls were probably coming from the nearby landfill. But it still looked pretty spectacular.)

I'd almost call the scene cheesy if it wasn't the handiwork of God—but it WAS God's handiwork—with an obvious dose of his humor.

And it was beautiful.

I knew it was a sign from God meant for me.

You see, years ago when my kids were young, they used to pester me with deep theological questions like, "How do I know God is real?" and "How is God with us if we can't see him?" and "When it rains, is that God's pee?"

Without much theological training, I tried my best to answer their questions. I explained that a dove symbolizes the

Holy Spirit, which is God's presence with us and in us, so they could look for birds in the sky for a reminder of that truth.

I'm pretty sure I earned a divine high-five for that answer because my kids were constantly on the lookout for birds in the sky so they could "see" that God was present. When they hit the teen years, they were much less excited about Holy Spirit bird sightings. And by "much less excited," I mean NOT.

But the week before, when Paige called me from college and I'd felt totally helpless talking through her anxiety about the end of semester projects and finals, she mentioned she'd been looking for birds in the sky.

"Why?" I'd asked.

She said, "Because it helps me remember God is always with me. Duh."

So there it was. My God sighting right in front of me, and the answer to the question I should have known: *God is with us. He is for us. He loves us. All of us. Always.*

And he wants an everyday relationship with us—in the good, the bad, and the mundane business of life.

We don't earn the right for God's help based on the severity of our needs. We don't earn the right for God's presence. Period.

Because we don't need to.

We have Jesus, and we have grace. And they're gifts.

In the chaos, in the challenge, in the heartbreak as well as the joy of life, we can discover the deepest gratitude and peace by remembering the promise of the gospel and that God is always with us every step of the way.

O come, O come, Emmanuel.

"Therefore the Lord himself will give you a sign: The virgin will conceive and give birth to a son, and will call him Immanuel" (which means "God with us") Isaiah 7:14. (NIV)

Digging Deeper—Devotions and Journaling

The stories I shared in this chapter happened in the weeks leading up to Christmas. Those are weeks that, every year, can find the beauty of the season between Thanksgiving and Christmas overshadowed by my busyness and to-do lists. I'm guessing the same thing can easily happen to you.

In the stress of it all we might forget the true meaning of the season of Advent: celebrating the birth of our Savior, as well as looking forward in eager anticipation to the coming of Christ's kingdom when he returns for his people.

Read and reflect on this Bible verse:

> "And the Holy Spirit helps us in our weakness. For example, we don't know what God wants us to pray for. But the Holy Spirit prays for us with groanings that cannot be expressed in words" Romans 8:26. (NLT)

Whether it's the Christmas season or another time of the year, journal about what's on your mind that's troubling you. Make a quick list, including both the big things and the irritating, seemingly unimportant things.

Now close your eyes and take a few minutes to breathe deeply and reflect on the list you wrote. Those things you listed—they bother you, so take that list to God in prayer. But rather than recite every item, ask the Holy Spirit to hear the groaning of your heart and intercede on your behalf. Allow yourself to rest in the peace, comfort, and trust of knowing your needs are heard by God.

Read and reflect on this Bible passage:

> "But when the Father sends the Advocate as my representative—that is, the Holy Spirit—he will teach you everything and will remind you of everything I have told you. I am leaving you with a gift—peace of mind and heart. And the peace I give is a gift the world cannot give. So don't be troubled or afraid" John 14:26-27. (NLT)

Do you ever have God sightings—moments you recognize something (or someone) as a sign from God? Journal about some recent examples. Is God sighting a habit in your life, or is it happenstance?

Up for a Challenge?

The month of December is a season of prolific list-making, but we often make "to-do" lists every week of the year. For every list you make—even your grocery shopping list—add the phrase "Seek his peace" to your list. Let this practice help you pay more attention to the presence of God in the midst of your busy activities.

"I've learned that sharing Jesus with people who have nothing is much easier than sharing Jesus with people who have everything."

—wisdom from a Ugandan pastor

Chapter 12

For the Love of God and Money and Other Comfortable Things

"...a time to get and a time to lose."

Late Winter 2017

Midway through my son Nate's second semester as a freshman in college, the balance in his checking account was 64 cents.

Despite being in the dorm and having a full meal plan, he'd managed to spend all of his graduation gift savings and part-time job earnings.

On what? Necessities such as books and school supplies, of course, and some worldly comforts like weekend ski trips and his decisions to drink fancy coffee and eat fast food instead of going to the dining hall.

The reality of his situation meant he'd have to back out of his plans for a spring break trip with friends. He'd already paid a small deposit for the trip, which he'd lose, and his backing out left his buddies needing to fill his spot in order to make the hotel stay affordable.

"This is so *awkward!*" he growled at me, clearly hoping I'd offer to bail him out of the situation. "What if my friends can't find someone else to go and now they all have to pay extra because of it?"

"That's not my problem to solve," I replied.

He grumbled a bit more, but never directly asked me for money. He knew better than to poke the bear, as that bear was already paying for most of his college expenses.

I knew this First World dilemma Nate was facing offered a valuable lesson he needed to learn. And although I was proud of myself for sharing some sage advice about how to manage his finances instead of bailing him out of the situation, I couldn't help but feel like a hypocrite.

I'm no expert in navigating financial burdens, but I've discovered that the issue won't be solved by just learning how to better manage money. It's a truth I learned several years ago as the result of an unforgettable conversation with a pastor from Uganda.

We were sitting next to each other at a ministry training workshop, and I learned that he was the pastor of a thriving church in a poor, war-torn village in Uganda. He was nearing the end of a two-month sabbatical spent trekking across the

United States to meet and learn from other successful pastors in his denomination.

He shared how blessed he'd been to meet with some well-known ministry leaders and how his eyes had been opened to so many things.

Assuming he was returning to his home country overflowing with amazing stories of ministry in America, I asked, "What's been the most valuable thing you've learned here?"

He paused, and his eyes filled with tears.

"I've learned that sharing Jesus with people who have nothing is much easier than sharing Jesus with people who have everything."

He went on to explain how our American culture of comfort and prosperity was a distraction, insulating us from having to truly rely on God. His experience in our culture made him realize how vibrant the faith of his Ugandan congregation was despite enduring war, persecution, and poverty.

"*All* we have is Jesus," he said, "He is our everything, and he's all we need. Being here has begun to suffocate my soul."

By this point he was weeping openly, grieving for the people of America and longing for his home.

Wow.

I haven't been able to shake that conversation ever since, and it still makes me squirm.

It made me realize the unsettling truth that I pursue worldly comfort and God as an entwined package.

A quest for wealth has never been my goal, but I've always pursued financial security and craved the feeling of safety that comes from knowing I have enough money to pay my bills, tithe without worry, and have enough in savings for emergencies.

I like feeling comfortable. I like feeling thankful for what I have. I like feeling good about being generous (especially when I have enough money to give to others). I like feeling the pride that comes from my husband and I working hard and providing for our family. I like feeling the peace of knowing that my kids (hopefully) won't be drowning in too much student loan debt after college.

And I really like the feeling of being able to throw an impulse item (or two, or three) into my cart when I'm at Target.

Somehow I've rationalized my quest for financial comfort as a commendable quality, since I'm certainly not idolizing excessive wealth or prosperity.

But I've started to wonder if I've idolized the comfort of money without even realizing it—seeking the satisfaction that comes from providing for myself and others.

I'm no stranger to experiencing extreme discomfort with my finances. I've been a broke college student working extra jobs to cover expenses beyond tuition. I've been a young, single mother who went to bed panicked about the likelihood of the daycare check bouncing. I know the feeling of dread when opening the mailbox and finding a collection letter.

And now with juggling the tuition and expenses of having two kids in college, the familiar sick worry about money constantly haunts my life once again.

I do trust that God will provide. He always has. And I know he always will. But I have to admit how much I hate the feeling of financial pressure and scrambling to make ends meet.

Perhaps this is a lesson I have to keep learning through painful experience, and this discomfort is a necessary reminder to seek comfort in God's provision instead of the balance in my bank account.

And perhaps I need to view financial discomfort not as a problem to overcome, but as an invitation to invest in the priority of my faith in Jesus.

Digging Deeper—Devotions and Journaling

Read and reflect on this Bible verse:

> *"The seed falling among the thorns refers to someone who hears the word, but the worries of this life and the deceitfulness of wealth choke the word, making it unfruitful" Matthew 13:22. (NIV)*

What financial pressures are weighing on your mind? Make a list of the challenges in your life you believe would be solved if you had more money.

Glance again at the list you just wrote and consider: How do you feel? Take your concern and that list of needs, wants, and desires to God in prayer. For several minutes close your eyes and breathe deeply and then, rather than recite the list to God, ask the Holy Spirit to intercede and give you peace about trusting God's provision and timing. Surrender these financial burdens, remembering that your needs are known by God.

Read and reflect on this Bible verse:

> *"The Lord makes some poor and others rich; he brings some down and lifts others up" 1 Samuel 2:7. (NLT)*

Describe a time you faced a seemingly insurmountable financial issue—and survived it. In what ways did you see God's provision in that situation? How did the experience impact your faith?

_____

_____

_____

_____

_____

_____

_____

_____

_____

_____

_____

_____

_____

Now describe a time you felt blessed with financial abundance. In what ways did you see God's provision in that situation? How did the experience impact your faith?

Read and reflect on this Bible passage:

"Command those who are rich in this present world not to be arrogant nor to put their hope in wealth, which is so uncertain, but to put their hope in God, who richly provides us with everything for our enjoyment. Command them to do good, to be rich in good deeds, and to be generous and willing to share. In this way they will lay up treasure for themselves as a firm foundation for the coming age, so that they may take hold of the life that is truly life" 1 Timothy 6:17-19. (NIV)

Think about instances over the last few months when you've been aware of someone else's need but hesitated to reach out. Journal what these instances are, and list ways you might be able to help—whether by giving time, talent, or treasure.

_____

_____

_____

_____

_____

_____

_____

_____

_____

_____

_____

Up for a Challenge?

Reflect on what you've written, and ask God to show you a specific way he'd like you to show generosity. Follow through by taking action!

No matter how
bad things get,
when the storm rages
and when the world
comes crashing down,

God has
a plan.

Do not be afraid—
just reach for
his hand. He will
not release
his grip.

Chapter 13

Surviving the Storm When the World Comes Crashing Down

"...a time to tear down and a time to build"

Fall 2015—Spring 2016

My daughter started struggling with anxiety and panic disorder during her sophomore year in college.

At first I thought it was just normal college stress, but when I got a call from my daughter's roommate that Paige was "not OK," I felt the world as I knew it begin to crash down around me.

Paige had always been the most emotionally steady of all five of my kids. Responsible and even-tempered, she was a hard worker and calm problem-solver—a drama-free, easygoing kid who seemed mature beyond her years.

But this time she was truly not OK, and it was not just normal stress. Thus began our journey into a territory called "mental illness" that I struggled to wrap my head around.

She was anxious—not crazy—I kept telling myself. She'll snap out of it and be fine.

After wrestling with doubt and denial, I then battled with guilt and fear. I wondered if I'd done something in her life that had caused this, and I was terrified what this meant for her future. The stigma of the words *mental illness* was so real and scary. I feared others would judge or reject her.

I wanted to fix it and dove into research to try to understand what might be causing my daughter's anxiety and panic attacks—and how we could make it go away. I hoped we could find a simple cure like changing her diet and having her take supplements; perhaps she just needed vitamin D from a good dose of sunshine.

In the meantime, I got her connected with an incredible therapist—a woman I knew and deeply trusted. The therapist was licensed to give counseling sessions through a webcam so my daughter could access her conveniently.

The more I researched, the more I began to understand today's huge epidemic of anxiety and depression—and how rampant it is with kids as well as adults. College is often the time the state of one's mental health is revealed. My daughter wasn't crazy, nor was she alone. But this problem was big and it was for real.

Her anxiety gave *me* anxiety, as I felt so utterly helpless and ignorant about how to help her.

So, naturally, once I'd gotten to the point of complete despair, I remembered to reach out to God.

Only in God's presence did I find comfort and relief. I was reminded that he had created her exactly as she was, and he doesn't make mistakes. I knew the path of her life was planned by him, and he was alongside her.

I shared with my daughter about how I'd found hope in God's presence, and we both journeyed in this truth for the next 10 months, discovering the meaning of "peace that passes all understanding."

Through the ongoing process of managing her condition, my daughter not only survived, she thrived. It was not easy. There were days she struggled. But she no longer tried to hide her anxiety and pretend everything was fine.

The diagnosis I'd once thought was life-shattering turned out to be the opposite. It gave her the freedom to pursue health and wholeness from a place of honesty. Her faith grew deeper and her sense of purpose and identity was reframed by rooting herself to Christ. And I realized she was stronger and more confident than ever.

Shortly before her diagnosis during her sophomore year, she'd been accepted into a prestigious international study-abroad program in which she would spend the second semester of her junior year on board a cruise ship traveling around the world. We allowed her to keep this trip a hopeful reality, something she could work toward and look forward to as she progressed in therapy.

As the study-abroad departure time grew closer, I started feeling my anxiety and fear increase. She'd be gone for four months, on a boat, visiting 11 countries. She'd be rooming with one of her best friends since childhood, which eased my worries somewhat—but I couldn't shake the uneasiness that I felt. I spoke with her therapist, and she assured me that Paige was fine to go. She'd also still be able to continue on with her therapy sessions as needed through internet webcam.

Despite my worry, Paige was thrilled to be going on this program abroad. She meticulously planned all the details herself, getting vaccinations and travel visas for the various countries as well as a scholarship and a student loan to help pay the expenses. She moved all of her things back home at winter break since she'd sublet her room for second semester.

On December 21, just 10 days before she was supposed to depart on the program's ship, my phone rang. It was my daughter, crying hysterically.

"I just got a call from the director," she sobbed. "They reviewed my health records and told me I'm unfit to sail! They're pulling me off the trip!"

And once again I felt the world as we'd known it begin to crash in around us. I told her to call her therapist immediately, and I would call the program director. We could surely work this out.

Despite a conference call which included the program's director and head doctor, myself, and Paige's therapist, they refused to change their decision.

Paige had filled out her medical background honestly, including her struggle and diagnosis with generalized anxiety disorder. Earlier in the fall a medical professional from the program had called her after reviewing her file to inquire if she was on any medication. When she said she was not, the medical professional recommended she get a prescription for anxiety "just in case."

Unfortunately, that advice was now the problem. When Paige submitted the final medical paperwork—including her new prescription which she had filled in early December—it raised a red flag. There was a strict rule that kids weren't allowed to go if they had been prescribed medication for a mental health issue within a certain time period before departure.

I was in shock. Paige's world had just been torn apart…all because of her anxiety diagnosis. It seemed cruel that a program that was so concerned about her well-being on the trip would brutally cast her off as a liability a mere 10 days before departure, leaving her behind to pick up the pieces of her life.

She had no college classes scheduled for second semester since her full course load would have occurred through the program on board the ship. She had no place on campus to live. Many of her friends were going abroad to various places second semester. She was alone and without a plan.

I was in full panic mode. What would this do to her? Would this spin her backward and cause her to spiral into a deep depression or anxiety-fueled breakdown? Would she now only see herself as a liability—unfit to be out in the world with her peers?

I cried. I raged. I begged God to make the people at the study-abroad program change their minds and tell us it was all a silly mistake. I dropped to the floor of my bedroom in utter despair and grief for what this could do to my daughter's mental health…and then I suddenly felt awash with God's peace.

It was as if I could hear him say, *I am here—and I have other plans. Better ones. Trust me, you'll see.*

At that moment my daughter pulled into the driveway, and I ran to hug her. I held her, and we cried for a minute. Then I told Paige that I believed that when things go so crazy off course it could only be the hand of God pointing to somewhere better. Her heartfelt response was, "I know. He's been telling me the same thing. I think he has a different adventure in mind for me."

A week later she found an international organization that placed volunteers in remote places all over the world to serve in impoverished areas. She was accepted into a 10-week program to teach elementary school in a remote village on the east coast of Fiji.

And on January 21, exactly one month after Paige had been disqualified as a liability for sailing around the world on her study-abroad program, we stood in the airport and hugged goodbye.

All of her belongings were packed in a large hiking pack that was almost the same size as she was. She looked like a tiny child on her first day of school. Excited but quite nervous, she turned to me as she got to the security line and said, "I've never traveled alone."

"You're not alone," I reminded her. "God is with you. He brought you on this journey for his purpose, and he is with you every step. Just reach for his hand and you'll know."

As I drove home from the airport, I briefly wondered if this was a good decision. She'd been turned away as a medical risk from a program on a well-equipped cruise ship with the security of staff doctors and psychologists aboard. Now she was venturing off across the world all alone. She'd be living in a grass hut in a poor village that had the barest of necessities.

But I had peace that it was God's plan.

Once she was in Fiji I heard from her weekly when she was able to get a local SIM card for her phone. She messaged me pictures of the mat she slept on, her bedding infested with bedbugs. Her legs were covered in festering sores and tropical ulcers from mosquito bites, and her hair was crawling with lice. She'd been having some bad headaches lately that made me worried.

But she had fallen in love with the kids she taught and the host family in her village with whom she had dinner most evenings. She called her host mom "Na" and host dad "Ta," and she felt loved and accepted. She was excited to be making a difference in people's lives.

On February 21, exactly one month after I'd said goodbye to her at the airport, I got an urgent message from her. My heart leaped into my throat as I read her words:

"Don't freak out, but there's a Category 5 tropical cyclone headed our way. We're securing the village. If things get too bad, we will evacuate to Suva. Pray for my family here."

I immediately went online to search for news about the storm, subscribing to every internet feed for weather in that part of the world. The radar introduced me to Severe Tropical Cyclone Winston—a giant mass of red and purple making its way toward Fiji. It was being called the "perfect storm"— unfolding the worst possible case scenario.

And it was aiming for a direct hit on Fiji, predicted to make landfall on the east coast of Fiji—exactly where my daughter's village was located.

Her world was about to come crashing down again—literally—and potentially right on top of her.

"Get out of the village! Get everyone out of the village! This storm is huge and coming right at you!" I quickly messaged her back. "Evacuate now!"

"We'll go if it gets bad enough," she wrote back. "Right now we're focused on keeping the villagers safe. Just pray. And don't panic if you don't hear from me because phone and internet lines on the whole island might be down."

I prayed like I've never prayed before. I also reached out to every group of prayer warriors I knew and asked them to pray.

In between praying I watched the weather radar with fascinated horror. The storm grew bigger and meaner. Severe Tropical Cyclone Winston had sustained wind speeds of 175 mph and gusts over 190 mph. It was now being labeled the most intense tropical cyclone to ever make landfall in the southern hemisphere—the second most intense storm ever recorded in the history of the world.

Perhaps it was shock, but I felt a deep peace I couldn't explain. I like to call it God, because I felt it with such certainty. This was all in his plan; he was holding Paige in the palm of his hand. She would endure the storm with him, and good would come. My heart held on to this.

For the next 24 hours I watched the news reports as Cyclone Winston hit the small island of Fiji, engulfing the entire country. As the storm passed I searched the aerial footage of the aftermath on the island. Paige's village was now nothing but a rubble of cinder blocks. The palm trees were bare. The grass huts the volunteers lived in were gone. I couldn't imagine how anyone had even survived.

She contacted me later that night, her voice calm but concerned. She and her team of eight volunteers had evacuated at the last minute and made it to a small youth hostel in Fiji's capital city of Suva. The storm had ripped the roof partially off right over their heads, and they had hunkered down all night under mattresses in the small lobby.

"Mom, I don't know if the people of my village are OK. The roads are washed out…we can't get to them. Please pray," she said, now crying softly.

I was so relieved she was alive and safe, but unsure what was next. I learned it would be at least a week or two until the airport was usable for commercial flights. I wouldn't be able to bring her home from this right now, and there was nothing I could do.

For the next several weeks we remained in steady contact. She and her team of volunteers were working with local agency relief efforts and doing online fundraising campaigns to help rebuild their village.

They were all living in one little bunk room in the hostel. They had small rations of fresh water and cans of beans, and they had all contracted some sort of stomach virus that made life even rougher. But every time I talked with Paige, she could only talk about her village and her desire to go back and help rebuild.

"I'm not coming home!" she declared. "I need to extend my stay because I need to get back to my village and show them I didn't leave them behind. I need to see my Na and make sure she's OK. God sent me here to serve, and they need me more than ever."

I wasn't going to argue with her direction from God, so we extended her stay for another month. She and her team were able to go back to the village in March, and they'd already raised enough in funding from donors to begin to rebuild.

The only structure that remained somewhat intact in the village was the school, which now housed the 200 homeless villagers. Despite the area's catastrophic loss of life, limb, livestock, crops, and homes, the stories being shared were ones of miraculous survival and gratitude.

Paige marveled at the resilience of these people and how they were still full of joy and hope. The kids still played in the puddles, and the men and women of the village went straight to the task of rebuilding their homes, singing the traditional Fijian songs of their heritage the whole time.

"When I saw my Na, she ran to me, screaming my name," Paige shared. "As she hugged me, she sobbed into my neck and kept saying, 'Thank you, thank you.' I asked what she was thanking me for and she said, 'For coming back to me, Lewa!' She was so happy that her whole family was safe. And she was also one of the lucky ones, because she still had some of her house left."

And with that, I suddenly realized why God had sent her there. She and the villagers had faced the storm and survived it. The world as they knew it had come crashing down around them—even the walls caved in. But not all was lost. Despite the terror of the cyclone and the hardships that resulted from it, love, hope, and peace remained.

They had each other, and they had God.

And I knew, without a doubt, this experience had taught my daughter a profound lesson about anxiety and God's goodness: No matter how bad things get, when the storms rage and the world comes crashing down, God has a plan. Do not be afraid—just reach for his hand. He will not release his grip.

It was a lesson she could truly understand only with the perspective gained from having lived through it.

And it was a lesson I, too, had needed to learn as a mother. The world as we know it will sometimes come crashing down; it's just how life works. Trusting God through the storm is the only way to survive it—especially if you're watching it all unfold as you sit helplessly on the other side of the planet.

Digging Deeper—Devotions and Journaling

Read and reflect on these Bible passages:

> "We are pressed on every side by troubles, but we are not crushed. We are perplexed, but not driven to despair. We are hunted down, but never abandoned by God. We get knocked down, but we are not destroyed" 2 Corinthians 4:8-9. (NLT)

> "Those who live in the shelter of the Most High will find rest in the shadow of the Almighty. This I declare about the Lord: He alone is my refuge, my place of safety; he is my God, and I trust him. For he will rescue you from every trap and protect you from deadly disease. He will cover you with his feathers. He will shelter you with his wings. His faithful promises are your armor and protection" Psalm 91:1-4. (NLT)

Recall storms in your life—times you felt as if your world was crashing in around you.(Perhaps you're experiencing that now in life.) How did you survive? Journal how you were able to experience God's peace and presence in the storm—if that's what happened for you. And if you're in the midst of a storm now, ask God to walk with you and give you refuge.

_____

_____

_____

_____

_____

Read and reflect on the following Bible verse:

"And the God of all grace, who called you to his eternal glory in Christ, after you have suffered a little while, will himself restore you and make you strong, firm and steadfast" 1 Peter 5:10. (NIV)

Recall a time in your life in which you faced rejection or disappointment. Was there something better in store that you're now able to see in hindsight? Journal about how something positive came from a negative situation in your life.

Up for a Challenge?

The next time your child faces a storm in life, pause before you jump in to remedy it. Ask God to show you what his plans are in the situation, and pray for his peace and guidance.

He still
held them
in the palm
of his hand
even though
they'd let
go of mine.

Chapter 14

A Warm Wind and New Season of Firsts

"…a time to embrace."

Late Spring 2017

As my kids have grown up, Mother's Day has taken on a new meaning.

It's no longer symbolized by breakfast in bed and an abundance of handmade cards and construction-paper flower creations from elementary-school art class.

These days, Mother's Day signals the end of the second semester of college and a brief return to a fullness of the nest as my kids make their way back home.

This year I delayed our official Mother's Day celebration for a few weeks because it offered the rare opportunity to embrace the sacred timing of all five of my kids coming home for a weekend together.

My stepdaughter, Faith, who graduated college nearly a decade ago is now married and the mother of two little boys of her own. She and her family live nearby and spend time with us often, giving me the joy of experiencing the next (and possibly the most precious) chapter of parenthood. They'd agreed to sleep over at the house for that night so we could all be under one roof together.

My stepson, Chris, who we'd tearfully said goodbye to a few years ago when he took a job across the country after graduating from college in our hometown, was back for a few days with his lovely new wife, Jessica. I hadn't seen him since the wedding several months before, and I was thrilled to spend a few days with both of them.

My daughter, Paige, was home from college, albeit briefly. She had plans to return in a few weeks for summer semester in pursuit of her goal to graduate with her double major by December. She'd been invited to join the staff of the international volunteer organization in which she'd served while in Fiji, and she was excited to consider an assignment somewhere on the other side of the world.

Fortunately, for the moment, she was still only an hour away and frequently showed up back home claiming she missed our dogs.

My son Nate was home from his freshman year of college with a shaggy unshaven face he was hoping to finally call a beard when he headed back to Montana in August. He'd be busy working to earn money over the summer, but at least he was back home and sleeping in his own bed for a few months.

And my youngest son, Caleb, the one left behind who'd watched all of his siblings take flight over the years, was still at home. But this was the summer before his senior year of high school, and next year at this time he'd be graduating.

And then the journey of letting go will begin again—for the last and final time.

But I didn't let my thoughts wander much beyond that moment because there was too much goodness to savor. For 24 hours my nest would be full—all of the kids under one roof, including their spouses and children.

I knew I'd sleep well with the peace and completeness of everyone at home.

We all sat around the backyard fire pit that evening, laughing together like old friends as everyone shared stories of the adventures they'd experienced over the past year. The daylight faded and the firelight illuminated the joy in their sweet faces as I looked around at these people—my people— who I loved more than anything.

I reveled in the holiness of the present.

I was in awe of these amazing humans, so full of life and dreams and new beginnings.

And I was in awe that God had given me the privilege of being their mother.

As the night carried on, I noticed the warmth of the spring breeze that had stirred up around us. My thoughts went back again to the final chapter of *Charlotte's Web* and the words from one of the baby spiders:

> *We're leaving here on a warm updraft. This is our moment for setting forth. We are aeronauts and we are going out into the world to make webs for ourselves.*

But this time I didn't cry. Because I was discovering that they weren't sad words that signified the end—they were words of joy that represented new beginnings and the fullness of life ahead.

I'd released my grip, but my kids weren't gone forever.

This was a new season of parenthood with a new normal that consisted of a steady rhythm of coming and going, of saying "goodbye" and "welcome home" again and again.

It was also more than a season of lasts. It was a new season of firsts—full of the excitement these kids had as they launched out into the world as their own brave, bold, and independent selves.

Nothing could separate them from my love or the love and presence of God.

He still held them in the palm of his hand even though they'd let go of mine.

That truth was the only thing I knew for certain beyond the current moment.

But it was enough. And it was something I could hold on to forever.

Thanks be to God.

His truth is enough.

Now

may the Lord of peace himself
give you his peace at all times
and in every situation.
The Lord be with you all.

2 Thessalonians 3:16 (NLT)

About the Author

Kami Gilmour is the author of *Release My Grip: Hope for a Parent's Heart as Kids Leave the Nest and Learn to Fly*, and co-author of *The Skinny on Parents*. She's also a popular writer for the *SoulFeed* blog and co-host of *They Say* podcast, where she muses about faith and parenthood and often has a tendency to overshare her hilarious (and slightly inappropriate) life adventures.

She is passionate about encouraging teens, young adults, and parents, and is the co-creator of SoulFeed care packages, which feeds college kids what matters most: their faith.

As a mother of three and stepmother of two teenage and young adult kids, she is a seasoned veteran of "letting go." Despite decades of parenting experience and her role as a sage advice-giver to millions of parents on the *SoulFeed* blog, she has yet to master the most basic organizational skills and exists in a state of perpetual chaos.

She and her husband, Tim, live in Colorado, and enjoy all things "mountain-y." They look forward to someday being able to park their cars in their own garage when their "almost grown and flown" kids stop using it as a storage unit.

You can read more from Kami Gilmour on her blog at soulfeed.com. To connect with her for speaking engagements, interviews, or other inquires, you can reach her at soulfeed@mylifetree.com or @KamiGilmour on Twitter.

Where will Jesus interrupt you?

Endless to-do lists...or a chance to slow down and pay attention to Jesus? When we invite Jesus to interrupt every moment in our lives—not just the quiet, calm ones—suddenly even hectic daily planning takes on a whole new purpose.

For books, Bibles, devotions, planners, and coloring experiences that move Jesus into EVERY corner of your life, visit...

JesusCenteredLife.com

    #JesusInterruption